The Amazing Animals

Coloring Storybook

by Cole Hughes

Test Color Page

The lion teaches us to be strong and brave. It has a loud roar and reminds us of the Lion of Judah in the Bible.

A lamb is a baby sheep. It is very soft and cute. Lambs teach us innocence, sacrifice, and gentleness.

The dove is a pretty, white and gray bird. It makes soft, gentle cooing sounds. Doves remind us of peace and love.

Fish live in water. They come in all different shapes and sizes. They can be colorful and beautiful. Fish played an important part in several well-known miracles.

The cow is a big, gentle animal that lives on farms. It provides us with milk to drink and reminds us of God's goodness to us.

The horse is strong and powerful.
Horses can remind us that good
triumphs over evil.

The donkey is known for being hardworking and patient. Donkeys remind us to help people, even though we may not receive recognition or praise.

The raven has black feathers and a loud caw. Ravens are scavengers. They eat whatever they can find. Ravens teach us that God provides for our needs.

Sheep have soft, fluffy wool. They are gentle and peaceful. They teach us to follow the Good Shepherd who takes care of us.

The goat is a sure-footed climber with curved horns and a beard! Goats eat almost anything, including weeds. These animals remind us about strength and sacrifice.

The bear is a large, powerful animal with fur. Bears remind us to be brave and treat others with respect.

The snake has a long, thin body and crawls on the ground. Snakes teach us about deception and temptation. They remind us of the importance of making good choices.

The eagle is a large and powerful bird. It has sharp talons and keen eyesight. Eagles remind us of strength, courage, and freedom.

The fox is clever and sneaky. It teaches us to use our minds to solve problems and overcome challenges.

The hen takes care of her chicks. Hens show us the importance of taking care of those who need help.

The hawk is a bird of prey. It can soar high in the sky. Hawks remind us that God watches over us and protects us.

The leopard is a big, strong cat. It is very agile. Leopards teach us about authority and goodness.

In ancient times, the camel was very valuable and used for transportation. Camels remind us of wealth and to use our resources wisely.

The wolf is a fierce hunter and a brave protector. Wolves teach us about protecting ourselves and others from danger.

The ostrich is a large bird with long, skinny legs and a long neck. It cannot fly, but it can run very fast! The ostrich reminds us to treat everyone with kindness, even if they are different.

God created all animals, and each one plays a valuable role in the world. God uses animals in the Bible to help us understand important ideas and learn different lessons.